Uncle John's
SUPREMELY SATISFYING
BATHROOM READER®

Uncle John's
SUPREMELY SATISFYING
BATHROOM READER®
The Miniature Edition™

RUNNING PRESS
PHILADELPHIA · LONDON

A Running Press® Miniature Edition™

Text excerpted from *Uncle John's Supremely Satisfying Bathroom Reader*®, copyright © 2001, by The Bathroom Readers' Press (a division of Portable Press). www.bathroomreader.com

All rights reserved under the Pan-American and International Copyright Conventions

Printed in China

Library of Congress Control Number: 2003103745

ISBN 978-0-7624-1711-7

This book may be ordered by mail from the publisher. Please include $1.00 for postage and handling.

But try your bookstore first!

Running Press Book Publishers
2300 Chestnut Street
Philadelphia, PA 19103-4371

Visit us on the web!
www.runningpress.com

Introduction

The tradition at the BRI is to list all those who have made this book possible. Impossible in such a short Introduction. Thank you to all of those who have contributed and to our loyal readers. Please enjoy this next miniature edition with Running Press.

Go with the Flow!

Uncle Al
Publisher, Portable Press
www.bathroomreader.com

Founding Fathers

You already know the names. Here's who they belong to.

Joyce C. Hall
Background: Hall started out selling picture postcards from a shoe box, but soon realized that greeting cards with envelopes would be more profitable.
Famous Name: He started a new company, Hallmark Cards, a play on

his name and the word for quality, and in 1916 produced his first card. But the innovation that made Hallmark so successful had little to do with the cards themselves—it was their display cases. Previously, cards were purchased by asking a clerk to choose an appropriate one. Hall introduced display cases featuring rows of cards that the customer could browse through. When he died in 1982, the company he founded in a shoebox was worth $1.5 billion.

Orville Gibson

Background: In 1881 Gibson got a job working in a shoe store in Kalamazoo, Michigan, but in his spare time, he built musical instruments from wood.

Famous Name: The instruments were so popular that he quit the shoe store, and in 1902 he incorporated the Gibson Mandolin and Guitar Company. Gibson died in 1918, two years before a Gibson employee invented a microphone that would fit inside the guitar, creating a prototype of the electric guitar.

Benjamin Franklin Goodrich Background: Goodrich was a surgeon in the Union Army, but when the bloody Civil War ended, he gave up medicine. In 1870 he bought the failing Hudson River Rubber Company and moved it from New York to Akron, Ohio, where it thrived.

Famous Name: In Akron, he produced his first actual product, a fire hose. The company went on to invent vinyl, synthetic rubber, and the first tubeless automobile tire, but not before changing its name to the B.F. Goodrich Company.

David Packard

Background: David Packard was an engineer with the General Electric Company. In 1938 he moved to California, where he renewed a friendship with William Hewlett. The two went into the electronics business, making oscillators that were smaller, cheaper, and better than anything else on the market.

Famous Name: Working from a small garage in Palo Alto, the Hewlett-Packard company earned $1,000 that first year. Today the garage is a state landmark: "The Birthplace of Silicon Valley." Packard died in 1996 leaving an estate worth billions.

Richard Warren Sears

Background: In 1886 Richard Sears managed a railroad office in rural Minnesota. As station agent, he had the opportunity to buy an unclaimed shipment of gold watches. He quickly sold them all . . . then ordered more. He sold those, too, then took his $5,000 in profits and moved to Chicago. **Famous Name**: Sears advertised for a watchmaker; the ad was answered by Alva Curtis Roebuck. Within two years they were partners, selling their wares via a mail-order catalog under the name . . . Sears, Roebuck & Co.

Paul Orfalea

Background: After graduating from the University of California at Santa Barbara, Orfalea opened a small copy shop next to a taco stand in nearby Isla Vista, starting with a single copy machine.

Famous Name: Business was brisk. He soon expanded the store, then branched out to the rest of California, and then all over the country. And all the stores bore his name, the nickname he got in college because of his curly red hair . . . Kinko's.

James Beauregard Beam

Background: Beam was running the distillery founded by his great-grandfather, Jacob Beam, until 1920, when the Volstead Act made the sale of alcoholic beverages illegal and he had to close the place down.

Famous Name: When Prohibition

was repealed in 1933, he celebrated
by building a new distillery and intro-
ducing a new bourbon, which he
named for himself . . . Jim Beam.

Random Facts

When the ground temperature is below freezing, it can't hail.

A New Yorker could eat out every night of their life and never eat at the same restaurant twice.

Odds that a phone number in L.A. is unlisted: 1 in 3.

Why isn't iron added to milk? Iron-fortified milk turns coffee green.

Armadillos can walk underwater to cross rivers.

Pele's Curse

Thinking of visiting Hawaii? Make sure that photos and memories are all you take home with you. Pele's watching . . .

Between a Rock and a Hard Place
Thousands of tourists visit Hawaii's

scenic Volcanoes National Park every year, and every year a little bit of the park leaves with them. Many visitors can't resist taking a few of the park's unique lava rocks or a handful of dark black sand as a reminder of their visit to the island. No harm done, right?

Try telling that to Timothy Murray, one of many who have suffered terrible luck since taking home a memento from the park. "My life literally fell apart," says Murray, 32, who naively scooped black sand into a pop bottle during a 1997 trip.

Upon returning home to Florida, Murray's luck took a sharp turn for the worse: He lost his job. His fiancée dumped him without warning. He began hitting the bottle. His pet died. FBI agents—who had received a tip from someone in Hawaii—arrested him for a minor computer copyright infringement violation. "The FBI agents said they never arrest people for what I did," says Murray. "They told me, 'You really must have pissed someone off.' After some research, I figured out who it was."

It was Pele.

Legend Has It . . .

Here's the legend: Of all the deities in Hawaiian lore, the most well known—and most feared—is Pele, the fiery-tempered volcano goddess who Hawaiians believe created their islands. Pele is the daughter of the Earth goddess Haumea. According to myth, Pele spent most of her youth learning to make and control fire. But she was wild and the sea goddess, Namaka, was the one who had to put out her mistakes. Haumea knew that Namaka would hunt Pele down and punish her, so she sent Pele to find a secluded home, where she could make as much fire as she pleased without disturbing anyone. Pele chose Hawaii—then only a tiny atoll— which she made to rise out of the sea in a storm of volcanic activity. But Namaka tracked Pele down and confronted her. Fire and water clashed in a violent brawl. Namaka got the upper hand and banished Pele to Hawaii's volcanoes forever.

The hot-tempered goddess jealously guards her domain and takes out her anger at Namaka on the hapless humans who dare cross her. Hawaiians say that before every major eruption, Pele appears as a withered old woman walking along remote back roads. Those who pass her by find their homes destroyed by hot magma. However, those who offer her a ride find that a river of molten lava has stopped inches from their property. Many park visitors have reported meeting an old woman who asks for a cigarette, lights it with a snap of her fingers, and then vanishes mysteriously. Though Pele may like to tease humans playfully at times, she is dead serious about one thing: don't steal her property, or else.

Hawaiian Punch

The stories of Pele's revenge on the tourists who make off with her rocks are many. Since pinching a few rocks, Denver business owner Larry Bell has needed emergency heart surgery, had his marriage nearly fall apart, seen his daughter plagued by mysterious health problems, and had to relocate his business. One Los Angeles lava thief who was building a house watched helplessly as her basement floor caved in, her interior walls bent peculiarly, a worker drove a nail through his wrist, and her father-in-law fell off the roof and broke several ribs—all in the weeks following her return from the park. According to such "victims," Pele in her wrath has made cars break down, brought down stock prices, torn Achilles tendons, and even steered lawnmowers over toes.

Homeward Bound

Can this horrible luck be reversed? Every day, shipments of contraband lava rocks, shells, and even old shoes filled with sand are delivered anonymously to the post offices and park stations around Volcanoes National Park. The packages come from all over the world, sometimes containing debris taken from the park decades earlier. Some former visitors are so terrified of Pele's curse that they return to the park in person just to make sure that their rocks are put back in the exact spot they were taken from. One letter contained a single grain of sand, which the writer found in the cuff of a pair of pants he had worn while walking on the beach. In another letter, addressed to "Queen Pele, Hawaii," the writer's plea was simple: "Oh, please stop punishing me!"

Road to Recovery

Most park rangers insist that there is no curse of Pele, that it's only natural that a small percentage of the many people who go through the park every year will suffer some misfortune after leaving. The rangers claim that the practice of returning rocks is culturally insensitive and a waste of their time.

But there's no fooling Timothy Murray. "You may have your doubts about Pele," he says. "But let me tell you, when these things happen, you are willing to be on your knees in front of anyone or anything. Since I sent the sand back, I've started getting my life back. That's all I know." Murray's message to future park visitors: Beware Pele's wrath. Leave the rocks alone.

Who Invented Daylight Saving Time?
Ben Franklin did. In 1784 he wrote
an essay suggesting that setting clocks
ahead in the spring and behind in the
fall would be a wise idea because it
would save expensive candles. But
the idea wasn't taken seriously until
1907 when a British builder named
William Willett was riding through
the countryside early one morning
and noticed that in spite of the full
daylight, all the cottages' curtains
were still drawn. It was a waste of

daylight, he thought, and he wrote a
pamphlet advocating that the nation
set its clocks ahead by 20-minute
increments on each of the four
Sundays in April, and set them back
on the four Sundays in October. A
bill introduced in Parliament in 1909
was roundly ridiculed, but the advent
of World War I brought a dire need
to conserve coal, so the British
Summer Time Act was passed in 1916.
It set the time ahead one hour in the
spring and back one hour in the fall.

The United States followed suit and enacted Daylight Saving Time in 1918 to conserve fuel for the war effort, but the measure was so unpopular that it was repealed in 1919. It was reinstated during World War II, again to conserve fuel, but when the war ended, some localities opted to continue observing it and some didn't. And those that did couldn't agree on when to set their clocks forward and back. On a single 35-mile stretch of highway between West Virginia and

Ohio, for example, a traveler could pass through no less than seven time changes. Confusion reigned.

Bus Stop

The transportation industry, led by the Greyhound Bus Company, lobbied hard to remedy the situation, and finally in 1966 Congress passed the Uniform Time Act. The law didn't make Daylight Saving Time mandatory, but said that individual states needed to observe it or not on a uniform basis.

Daylight Saving Time is now observed in about 70 countries around the world.

Note: It's singular, not plural—it's Daylight Saving, not Daylight Savings. Why? We're saving daylight. According to the Department of Transportation, the United States saves about 1% of its energy every day DST is in effect. Maybe that makes it worth the effort for Americans to change three billion timepieces twice a year.

Why Are There Twenty-Four Hours in a Day?

The standard started with the ancient Sumerians, who also invented the first known system of writing. Their mathematical system was based on the number 12, just as ours is based on the number 10. The Sumerians, it is surmised, counted not the 10 digits of the hands, but the 12 segments of the 4 fingers on each hand. Twelve was considered a magical number because it is the lowest number with the greatest number of divisors—it is easily split into half or thirds or quarters or sixths, whereas 10 can only be cut in half or into fifths.

Their systems of weights, measures, and money were all based on 12, and so was their system of time. It was the Sumerians who first divided the day into 12 parts, with each segment equal to 2 of our hours. Later, the Egyptians modified the system by dividing the day into 24 segments. And in case you were wondering, the

Babylonians are responsible for our current system of having 60 minutes in an hour and 60 seconds in a minute.

Why Are There Time Zones?

You can thank the railroads for this one. Before the transcontinental railroads, there were no time zones. Noon in any city was whenever the sun reached the meridian of that particular place. Time actually varied by one minute for every 13 miles traveled, and cities only a few hundred miles apart had times that were different, which made scheduling trains very difficult. For example, when it was noon in Chicago, it was 12:31 in Pittsburgh, 12:17 in Toledo, 11:50 in St. Louis, and 11:27 in Omaha. At one time, U.S. railroads had nearly 300 different time zones. This lack of consistency wasn't just inconvenient, it was dangerous. The possibility of train wrecks increased dramatically by the conflicting schedules.

Something had to be done—not locally—but on a global basis.

By 1847 Great Britain had a unified time system, which meant they had a single time zone across the entire country. That was fine for the small island nation. But it wasn't as easy in North America—the United States and Canada cover some 60 degrees of longitude.

In 1872 the Time-Table Convention was founded in St. Louis to look for a solution. Charles Dowd, a school

principal from New York, [illegible]
mended that the U.S. set u[illegible]
time zones, and brought hi[illegible]
Congress. Most lawmakers[illegible]
with the idea, but were afr[illegible]
would upset their constitue[illegible]
bill was stalled on the Hou[illegible]
more than a decade.

Standard Sanford

It wasn't until Sir Sanford[illegible]
well-respected Canadian [illegible]
engineer, brought a specifi[illegible]

to Washington that the idea began to take hold. His idea: because there are 24 hours in a day, divide the Earth's 360 degrees by 24, which will create 24 equal time zones separated by 15 degrees.

In 1882 the Standard Time system was finally adopted, officially dividing the United States into four time zones—Eastern, Central, Mountain, and Pacific. At noon on Sunday, November 18, 1883—a day that became known as "the day with two

noons"—the railroads set their clocks
to this system.

On October 13, 1884, leaders from
25 nations gathered at the International
Meridian Conference in Washington,
D.C., divided the world into 24 time
zones, with Greenwich, England,
chosen to be the "prime meridian."
The day would begin there and time
would change by one hour for each
15 degrees traveled from that point.
Slowly but surely the rest of the
world adapted to the new time zones.

Some applauded it, others rejected it —
but because the railroads were the
primary means of transportation and
shipping at the time, people had little
choice.

Still, it wasn't until 1918 that
Congress got around to making the
Standard Time Act a matter of law —
a law made, coincidentally, in
conjunction with passing the first
Daylight Saving Time Act.

Random Facts

World's largest manufacturer of
female apparel: Mattel (They make
Barbie's clothes.)

The average American worker
receives 201 phone, paper, and e-mail
messages per day.

Heads up: Raindrops fall as fast as
22 mph.

Only 6% of coupons printed are ever redeemed.

Number one health complaint Americans report to the doctors: insomnia.

Classic Hoaxes

The BRI library is full of books on hoaxes. We love them. It's amazing how many times people have pulled off clever scams . . . and gotten away with it. Here are a few of our favorites.

The Mysterious Chicken of the Apocalypse

Background: In a small village near Leeds, England, in 1806, a hen laid an egg that had the words "Christ is Coming," inscribed in black on its surface. The hen's owner, a woman named Mary Bateman, explained that God had come to her in a vision and told her that the hen would lay a total of 14 such eggs, at which point the world would be destroyed in the apocalypse. Only the holy would survive to live with Christ in heaven; everyone else was condemned to burn in hell.

But there was some good news: God had given Bateman special slips of paper sealed with the inscription "J.C." Anyone possessing one of these slips would be automatically admitted into heaven . . . and Mary Bateman was willing to part with the papers for a shilling apiece.

"Great numbers visited the spot, and examined these wondrous eggs, convinced that the day of judgement was near at hand," Charles Mackay writes in *Extraordinary Popular Delusions and the Madness of Crowds*. "The believers suddenly became religious, prayed violently, and flattered themselves that they repented them of their evil courses." By the time the 14th and final egg was about to be laid, more than 1,000 people had coughed up a shilling to be admitted into heaven.

Exposed: A doctor who was skeptical of the story traveled to Leeds to investigate the eggs in person. When he discovered that the messages had been written on them with corrosive ink, he informed the local authorities, who raided the tavern where the chicken was being kept . . . just as Mary Bateman was cruelly shoving an inscribed egg into the hen to "lay" later that day.

Bateman was sent to jail but was soon released. No longer able to make a living in the prophecy business, she became an abortionist, which was illegal, and for which she was later hanged.

The Amityville Horror

Background: In 1974 a man named Ronald DeFeo murdered his parents and four siblings as they slept in their home in Amityville, New York. He was convicted of the crimes and sentenced to six consecutive life sentences in prison.

The "murder house" was later sold for a song to a struggling couple named George and Kathy Lutz, who moved in a week before Christmas in 1975. Twenty-eight days later, they moved out, claiming the house was haunted—and that the evil spirits that had driven them away probably also caused DeFeo to murder his entire family. Their story inspired the 1977 best-selling book *The Amityville Horror*, and the hit film that premiered in 1979.

Exposed: In 1979 Ronald DeFeo's defense attorney William Weber filed a lawsuit against the Lutzes, accusing them of fraud and breach of contract, claiming that they reneged on an agreement to collaborate with Weber on the book. So where did the haunted house story come from? In an interview with the Associated Press, Weber admitted that he and the Lutzes had "concocted the horror story scam over many bottles of wine."

Sober Sue

Background: One afternoon in 1908, the managers of Hammerstein's Victoria Theater on Broadway marched a woman onstage during intermission and offered $1,000 to anyone in the audience who could make the woman —introduced as "Sober Sue"—laugh. When no one in the audience succeeded in getting Sober Sue to even crack a smile, the theater managers upped the ante by inviting New York's top comedians to try.

Over the next several weeks, just about every headlining comedian in New York City performed their best material in front of Sober Sue, hoping to benefit from the publicity if they were first to get her to laugh. Everyone failed, but Sober Sue became one of Broadway's top theater attractions.

Exposed: It wasn't until after she left town that Sober Sue's secret finally leaked out: Her facial muscles were paralyzed—she couldn't have laughed even if she had wanted to. The Victoria Theater had cooked up the "contest" to trick New York's most famous—and most expensive—comedians into performing their routines for free.

Random Facts

Seeing is believing: Even a blind chameleon will change its color to match its surroundings.

Most common first name in the world: Muhammad. Most common last name: Chang.

Take a letter: Once you file something, there's a 98% chance you'll never look at it again.

Amen is the same in more languages than any other word. Taxi is second.

Let freedom ring: About half the world's telephones are in the U.S.

Incredible Animal Facts

Sit. Fetch. Roll over. Even more interesting than watching animals perform tricks we teach them is watching what they do naturally. This list of truly amazing facts about animals was compiled by BRI staffer Taylor Clark.

• The world's longest earthworms — found only in a small corner of

Australia—can grow to as long as 12 feet and as thick as a soda can.

• Ancient Romans trained elephants to perform on a tightrope.

• Squids have the largest eyes in nature—up to 16 inches across.

• Australia's mallee bird can tell temperature with its tongue, accurate to within two degrees.

• Three-toed sloths sleep 20 hours a day and spend most of their days upside down.

• Most kangaroo rats never drink water.

• The chamois—a goatlike mountain antelope—can balance on a point of rock the size of a quarter.

• Robins become drunk after eating holly berries and often fall off power lines.

- Octopus eyes resemble human eyes — the U.S. Air Force once taught an octopus to "read" by distinguishing letterlike shapes.

- A woodpecker's beak moves at a speed of 100 mph.

- By using air currents to keep it aloft, an albatross may fly up to 87,000 miles on a single feeding trip without ever touching the ground.

That's more than three times around the Earth.

- Polar bears are so perfectly insulated from the cold that they spend most of their time trying to cool down.

- Whales can communicate with each other from over 3,000 miles away (but the message takes over an hour to get there).

- Domesticated elephants have

learned to stuff mud into the cowbells around their necks before sneaking out at night to steal bananas.

• A mouse has more bones than a human.

They Went Thataway

We're not just fascinated by the way famous people live, we're fascinated by the way they die, too. Here are a few stories from our BRI files.

Mary Todd Lincoln

Claim to Fame: Widow of President Abraham Lincoln

How She Died: In bed with "Mr. Lincoln."

Postmortem: Mrs. Lincoln's life was filled with tragedy: Her son Tad died from tuberculosis in 1850 when he was only 3; her son Willie died of typhoid fever in 1862 when he was 11; her husband was assassinated in 1865; and her 18-year-old son Thomas died in 1871. Only one of her children,

Robert Lincoln, survived into adulthood.

Mary Lincoln never recovered from the shock of her husband's death, and her son Thomas' death sent her completely over the edge. She suffered from hallucinations and by 1875 was so disturbed that she attempted suicide. Robert had her committed to an asylum that very night.

Four months later, she was released and sent to live with her sister in Illinois, and in June 1876, a jury ruled that she had re-gained her sanity.

In 1879 Mrs. Lincoln's health began to deteriorate. By now reclusive and nearly blind, she spent most of the last 18 months of her life locked in her bedroom, where she slept on one side of the bed because she was convinced that her husband was sleeping on the other side. She died on July 16, 1882, at the age of 63, after suffering a stroke.

John Denver

Claim to Fame: A singer and songwriter, Denver shot to fame in the 1970s with hits like "Rocky Mountain High" and "Take Me Home, Country Road."

How He Died: He crashed his own airplane.

Postmortem: Denver was a lifelong aviation buff and an experienced pilot. He learned to fly from his father, an ex-Air Force pilot who made his living training pilots to fly Lear Jets.

Denver had just bought an aerobatic plane known as a Long-EZ shortly before the crash and was still getting used to flying it. According to the report released by the National Transportation Safety Board, he needed an extra seatback cushion for his feet to reach the foot pedals, but when he used the cushion he had trouble reaching the fuel tank selector handle located behind his left shoulder. The NTSB speculates that he took off without enough fuel. When one of his tanks ran dry and the engine lost power, Denver accidentally stepped on the right rudder pedal while reaching over his left shoulder with his right arm to switch to the other fuel tank, and crashed the plane into the sea.

Final Irony: Denver's first big success came in 1967, when he wrote the Peter, Paul, and Mary hit "Leaving on a Jet Plane."

L. Ron Hubbard

Claim to Fame: Science-fiction writer and founder of the Church of Scientology

How He Died: No one knows for sure.

Postmortem: Hubbard founded his church in 1952. The larger it grew and the more money it collected from followers, the more controversial it became. A British court condemned Scientology as "immoral, socially obnoxious, corrupt, sinister, and dangerous;" a Los Angeles court denounced it as "schizophrenic and paranoid."

Hubbard had a lot of enemies in law-enforcement agencies in the U.S. . . . the IRS suspected him of skimming millions in church funds. For a time he avoided prosecutors by sailing around the Mediterranean, and from 1976 to 1979 he lived in hiding in small desert towns in Southern California. Then in 1980 he vanished. He didn't resurface until January 25, 1986, when someone called a funeral home in San Luis Obispo, California, and instructed them to pick up a body from a ranch about 20 miles north of town. The corpse was identified as Lafayette Ronald Hubbard.

The FBI's fingerprint files confirmed that the man really was Hubbard. The official cause of death: a cerebral hemorrhage. But a "certificate of religious belief" filed on behalf of Hubbard prevented the coroner from conducting an autopsy, so we'll never really know.

Random Facts

Rats can't vomit, which is why they are so susceptible to poison.

In the 1700s, trappers could get a dollar for a buckskin. Hence the term buck.

But don't drink it: Lemon Pledge has more lemons than Country Time Lemonade.

The world has been at peace only 8% of the time over the last 3,500 years.

Not again: 15% of drivers get 76% of all traffic tickets.

Familiar Phrases

Here are the origins to some common phrases.

Win Hands Down

Meaning: To win by an enormous margin.

Origin: If a racehorse jockey is so far ahead of the competition that there is no danger he will be passed again, he can drop the reins—and his hands—and let the horse finish the race without spurring it on.

Baker's Dozen

Meaning: Thirteen—one more than a dozen.

Origin: In the Middle Ages, bakers who sold loaves of bread that were lighter than the legal weight were subjected to harsh penalties. To prevent being accused of cheating on the weight, bakers would often give away an extra loaf with every dozen.

Clean as a Whistle
Meaning: Exceptionally clean or smooth.
Origin: This phrase appeared at the beginning of the 19th century, describing

The world has been at peace only 8% of the time over the last 3,500 years.

Not again: 15% of drivers get 76% of all traffic tickets.

Familiar Phrases

Here are the origins to some common phrases.

Win Hands Down

Meaning: To win by an enormous margin.

Origin: If a racehorse jockey is so far ahead of the competition that there is no danger he will be passed again, he can drop the reins—and his hands—and let the horse finish the race without spurring it on.

Baker's Dozen

Meaning: Thirteen—one more than a dozen.

pened to meet, especially the fiercest and most territorial creature in the land—the bear.

Bet Your Bottom Dollar

Meaning: It's a sure thing; to bet everything you have.

Origin: Just as they do today, 19th-century poker players would keep their betting chips—or "dollars"—in high stacks at the table, taking from the top when betting. When a hand was so good that a player wanted to wager the entire stack, they would pick up or push the stack by the bottom chip—literally betting with their bottom dollar.

To Fight Fire With Fire
Meaning: To respond in like manner; a desperate measure.
Origin: In order to extinguish huge prairie and forest fires in the early West, desperate American settlers would sometimes set fire to a strip of land in the path of the advancing fire

and then extinguish it, leaving a barren strip with nothing for the approaching fire to feed on. Although effective, this tactic was —and still is—extremely dangerous, as the backfire itself can get out of control.

To Get One's Goat

Meaning: To aggravate.

Origin: Hyperactive racehorses were often given goats as stablemates because their presence tended to have a calming effect on the horses. After

the horse became attached to
goat, it got very upset when i
panion disappeared—making
poorly on the track. In the 19th
when a devious gambler want
horse to lose, he would get the
goat and take it away the nigh
the race, thus agitating the hor

In the Nick of Time
Meaning: Without a second to
Origin: Even into the 18th cent
some businessmen still kept tra

transactions and time by carving notches — or nicks — on a "tally stick." Someone arriving just before the next nick was carved would arrive in time to save the next day's interest — in the nick of time.

Make Money Hand Over Fist

Meaning: Rapid success in a business venture.

Origin: Sailors through the ages have used the same hand-over-hand motion when climbing up ropes, hauling in nets, and hoisting sails. The best seamen were those who could do this action the fastest. In the 19th century, Americans adapted the expression "hand over fist"—describing one hand clenching a rope and the other deftly moving above it—to suggest quickness and success.

Random Facts

Whales dream.

President Busch: In a survey, U.S. children 8–12 could name more brands of beer than presidents.

Grocer's dozen: 90% of the world's food crops come from only 12 species of plants.

Aristotle stuttered.

Shut up! Giraffes have no vocal chords. How do they communicate? With their tails.

The House Call of a Lifetime

Every collector has a Holy Grail that they hope to find at a yard sale or a flea market someday. Baseball card collectors dream of finding an original Honus Wagner; book collectors hope to spot a copy of Edgar Allan Poe's

The Tamerlane gathering dust on a bookstore shelf. Here's the story of an amateur antique collector who found what he was looking for.

The Perfect Storm

One winter in the early 1980s, a two-day snowstorm knocked out telephone service to much of the village of East Hampton, New York. One of the people sent out into the snow to restore service was cable repairman Morgan MacWhinnie.

MacWhinnie was just finishing repairing an underground cable when an old man wearing slippers and a bathrobe came out of a run-down clapboard house and asked him to check the phones inside. MacWhinnie wanted to move on to his next repair call, but he decided it would be quicker to humor the old man than it would be to argue with him. So he went into the house.

Diamonds in the Rough

The old man turned out to be a pack rat. He had old aluminum TV dinner trays stacked to the ceiling in the kitchen, and mountains of trash in other parts of the dark, dusty house. MacWhinnie checked the extension in the kitchen; it had a dial tone. Then the old man insisted that he check the extension in the bedroom, too.

MacWhinnie wanted to leave, but the old man was insistent, so he let the man show him the way to the

upstairs room. As MacWhinnie made his way through the cluttered dining room, he was surprised to see what appeared to be an antique tea table and a matching bonnet-top highboy chest of drawers poking out of the dust and debris. Then, after he checked the extension in the bedroom (it was fine) and prepared to leave, he saw a matching drop-leaf dining table next to the front door.

Newport Style

As it turns out, MacWhinnie's hobby was collecting antiques. He knew a lot about 18th-century American furniture, and he was almost certain the pieces were valuable. In fact, he suspected they were made in Newport, Rhode Island, in the 1780s, the period considered the golden age of the Newport style. If he was right, the furniture was worth a lot of money, but he had no way of knowing for sure.

The old man told MacWhinnie that the furniture belonged to his landlady, a woman named Caroline Tillinghast. MacWhinnie called her and told her he thought the pieces were valuable and asked if she'd consider selling them. She said no—the house was a rental property, and she needed the furniture for the tenants.

MacWhinnie let the matter drop, but he never forgot what he saw that day.

Second Try

Ten years later, MacWhinnie happened to tell his story to an antiques dealer named Leigh Keno. (Does the name sound familiar? He and his twin brother Leslie appear regularly on the PBS TV series *Antiques Roadshow*.) When he heard MacWhinnie's story, Keno thought the pieces must be reproductions but agreed that they were worth a look just in case, so they called Tillinghast to see if she would let them come over and examine the furniture. Yes, she told them, and now was a good time, because the old man had recently passed away, and she was having the house cleaned for new tenants.

The Real Deal

MacWhinnie was right — the pieces were genuine. They turned out to be the work of John Goddard, considered the most talented cabinetmaker of the period. Finally, nearly a decade after MacWhinnie had asked her the first time, Tillinghast agreed to put the antiques up for sale. She believed they were worth "in excess of $25,000"—and she was right. A few weeks, later Keno brokered the sale to a collector for $1 million. As for MacWhinnie, he and Keno split the hefty commission 50-50.

Random Facts

Porcupines are good swimmers . . . their quills are full of air.

Disney World is twice the size of Manhattan.

Doctors in the 1700s prescribed lady-bugs, taken internally, to cure measles.

In pro Ping-Pong, if players use white balls, they can't wear white shirts. Why? Can't see 'em.

Poison oak is not an oak and poison ivy is not an ivy. Both are members of the cashew family.

An Uplifting Story

Our long-promised history of the bra
may seam padded, but it is contoured
especially for bathroom readers.
Thanks for your support.

Mother of Invention
Who invented the bra? Through the
1800s, a number of people patented
items of intimate apparel for women,
but most were just extensions of the
corset. In 1893 Marie Tucek was

granted a patent on a crude "breast supporter," which had a pocket for each breast, straps that went over the shoulders, and a hook-and-eye fastener in the back.

But the modern bra was really born 20 years later. The fashion of the early 1910s was to flatten the breasts for a slim, boyish figure; the fashion also favored plunging necklines. In 1913 a Manhattan debutante named Mary Phelps Jacobs became frustrated when her chest-flattening corset kept peaking out above her plunging neck-line. "The eyelet embroidery of my corset-cover kept peeping through the roses around my bosom," she wrote in her autobiography, *The Passionate Years*. The sheerness of her Paris evening gown was ruined by the lumpy, bulky corset.

What's a debutante to do?
In frustration, she and her maid designed an undergarment made of two handkerchiefs and some ribbons

that were pulled taut. "The result was delicious. I could move more freely, a nearly naked feeling, and in the glass I saw that I was flat and proper." Showing off her invention in the dressing rooms of society balls, she had her friends begging for brassieres of their own. Jacobs actually sewed and gave away many bras as gifts. But when strangers started accosting her, requesting the brassieres and offering money, Jacobs went to see a patent attorney (she had her maid model the garment discreetly over the top of her uniform).

A patent was granted and Jacobs opened a small manufacturing facility. She called her invention the "backless brassiere." It was the first ladies undergarment to dispense with corset-stiffening whalebone, using elastic instead. Jacobs sold a number of her brassieres under the name "Caresse Crosby," but for all her ability as a designer, she had no marketing instincts. Sales were flat, and she soon shelved the business.

A few years later, she bumped into an old boyfriend who happened to mention the fact that he was working for the Warner Brothers Corset Company. Jacobs told him about her invention and at his urging, showed it to his employers. They liked it so much they offered to buy the patent for $1,500. Jacobs took the money— she thought it was a good deal. So did Warner Brothers Corset Company— they went on to make some $15 million from Jacobs' invention.

Maidenform

Ida and William Rosenthal, two Russian immigrants, came to America penniless and set up a dressmaking business in New York with a partner, Enid Bissett. They were constantly dissatisfied with the way dresses fit around the female bosom, so in frustration—and perhaps in rebellion to the popular flat-chested look of the flapper—they invented the first form-fitting bra with separate "cups." And since all women are not built equally,

Ida invented cup "sizes."

The Rosenthals gave up the dress shop in 1922 and started the Maidenform Brassiere Company with a capital investment of $4,500. Four years later, they had 40 machines turning out mass-produced bras. Forty years later, they had 19 factories producing 25 million bras annually. Some of their innovations:

• The "uplift bra," patented in 1927.

- The "training bra" (no definitive word on what they were in training for).

- The "Chansonette bra," introduced in 1949. It had a cone-shaped cup stitched in a whirlpool pattern. The bra, which never changed shape, even when it was removed, was quickly dubbed the "Bullet Bra." Over the next 30 years, more than 90 million were sold worldwide.

When William died in 1958, Ida carried on and continued to oversee the company until her death in 1973 at the age of 87. The Maidenform corporation, which started with 10 employees, now has over 9,000.

Playtex

Another major contributor to the development of the bra was Abram Nathaniel Spanel, an inventor with over 2,000 patents (including one for a garment bag designed so that a vacuum cleaner could be hooked up to it to suck out moths). In 1932 Spanel founded the International Latex Corporation in Rochester, New York, to make latex items such as bathing caps, slippers, girdles, and bras, sold under the name Playtex.

Playtex was very aggressive with its advertising. In 1940—an era when underwear ads in print publications were primarily discreet line drawings—Playtex placed a full-page ad in *Life* magazine with photos of models wearing Playtex lingerie alongside a mail-in coupon. Women responded: 200,000 sales were made from the ad. And in 1954 Playtex became the first company to advertise a bra and girdle on TV. Those garments—the Living Bra and Living Girdle—remained part of the line for 40 years.

In 1965 Playtex introduced the Cross Your Heart Bra. Today it remains one of the best-known brands in the United States and is the second best-selling brand of Playtex bra, with the 18-Hour Bra filling out the top spot.

Howard Hughes

The tycoon and film producer also had his hand in creating a bra. In 1941 he was making a movie called *The Outlaw*, starring his 19-year-old "protégé," Jane Russell. Filming was going badly because the bras Russell wore either squashed her breasts or failed to provide enough support to prevent her from bouncing all over the screen.

According to legend, Hughes designed an aerodynamic half-cup bra, so well reinforced that it turned Russell's bosom into a veritable shelf. Censors had a fit. 20th Century Fox postponed the release date due to the controversy. Millions of dollars stood to be lost, so rather than back down, Hughes went all out. He had his people phone ministers, women's clubs, and other community groups to tell them exactly how scandalous this film was. That prompted wild protests.

Crowds of people insisted the film be banned. The publicity machine launched into full gear, and when the film was finally released, it was a guaranteed hit.

On opening night, Hughes hired skywriters to decorate the Hollywood skies with a pair of large circles with dots in their centers. Jane Russell, an unknown before the film, became a star overnight. Years later she revealed in her autobiography that she had found Hughes's bra so uncomfortable that she had only worn it once . . . in the privacy of her dressing room. The one she wore in the movie was her own bra. No one—not even Hughes—was the wiser.

The Very Secret Bra

An inflatable bra introduced in 1952, it had expandable air pockets that would help every woman achieve "the perfect contour." The bra could be discreetly inflated with a hidden hand pump. Early urban myth: these inflatable bras sometimes exploded when ladies wore them on poorly pressurized airplanes.

The Jog Bra
Hinda Miller and Lisa Lindahl were friends who enjoyed jogging but didn't like the lack of support their normal bras offered. Lingerie stores had nothing better to offer them, so they decided to make their own. In 1977 they stitched together two jock straps and tested it out—it worked. Their

original prototype is now displayed in the Smithsonian. In 1978 the two inventors sold $3,840 worth of their bras to sporting apparel stores. In 1997 Jogbra sales topped $65 million.

The Wonderbra
Originally created in 1964 by a Canadian lingerie company named Canadelle, the Wonderbra was designed to lift and support the bust-line while also creating a deep plunge and push-together effect, without

compressing the breasts. Even naturally flat-chested women could achieve a full-figured look. The bra was popular in Europe but wasn't even sold in the United States because of international licensing agreements.

In 1991 fashion models started wearing Wonderbras they had purchased in London. Sara Lee Corporation (yes, the cheesecake company), who by then had purchased Playtex, bought the license to the Wonderbra and began marketing it aggressively. They spent $10 million advertising the new product, and it paid off. First-year sales peaked at nearly $120 million. By 1994 the Wonderbra was selling at the rate of one every 15 seconds for a retail price of $26.

Random Facts

Football has more rules than any other American sport.

Why is honey so easy to digest? Because it's already been digested by the bee.

Ladybugs are named after the Virgin Mary; they used to be called "the beetles of our Lady."

Only female ducks quack; the males coo, hoot, honk, and grunt, but they don't quack.

The notebooks used by Marie and Pierre Curie are still too radioactive to be handled safely.

"The Blast Blasted Blubber Beyond All Believable Bounds"

We at the BRI are always on the lookout for great urban legends. For years the tale of the Exploding Whale has floated around the Internet. But it's not an urban legend — it's 100% true. Here's the story:

A Whale of a Problem

How do you get rid of a 45-foot-long

stinking dead whale? That was the bizarre question George Thornton had to answer on the morning of November 12, 1970. A few days earlier, an eight-ton rotting sperm whale carcass had washed ashore on a Florence, Oregon, beach, and the responsibility fell on Thornton — assistant highway engineer for the Oregon State Highway Division — to remove it. His options were limited. He couldn't bury the rapidly decomposing corpse on site because the tides would soon uncover it, creating a health hazard for beachgoers. And because of the whale's overpowering stench, his workers refused to cut it up and transport it elsewhere. He also couldn't burn it. So what could he do? Thornton came up with an unbelievable solution: blow the whale up with dynamite.

Whale Watching

Thornton's expectation was that the whale's body would be nearly disintegrated by the explosion, and he assumed that if any small chunks of whale landed on the beach, scavengers like seagulls and crabs would consume them. Indeed, many seagulls had been hovering around the corpse all week.

Thornton had the dynamite placed on the leeward side of the whale, so that the blast would hopefully propel the whale pieces toward the water. Thorton said, "Well, I'm confident that it'll work. The only thing is we're not sure how much explosives it'll take to disintegrate the thing." He settled on 20 cases—half a ton of dynamite.

As workers piled case upon case of explosives underneath the whale, spectators swarmed around it to have their pictures taken—upwind, of course—in front of the immense carcass, right near a massive gash where someone had hacked away the beast's lower jaw. Even after officials herded the crowds a full quarter of a mile away for safety, about 75 stubborn spectators stuck around, most of them equipped with binoculars and tele-photo lenses. After almost two hours of installing explosives, Thornton and his crew were finally ready to blow up a whale. He gave the signal to push in the plunger.

Thar She Blows!

The amazing events that followed are best described through the eye of a local TV news camera that captured the episode on tape. The whale suddenly erupts into a 100-foot-tall plume of sand and blubber. "Oohs" and "aahs" are heard from the bystanders as whale fragments scatter in the air. Then, a woman's voice breaks out of the crowd's chattering: "Here come pieces of . . . WHALE!" Splattering noises of whale chunks hitting the ground grew louder, as onlookers scream and scurry out of the way. In the words of Paul Linnman, a Portland TV reporter on the scene, "The humor of the entire situation suddenly gave way to a run for survival as huge chunks of whale blubber fell everywhere."

For several minutes after the blast, it rained blubber particles. Fortunately, no one was hurt by the falling chunks, but everyone—and everything—on the scene was coated with foul-smelling, vaporized whale. The primary victim of the blubber was an Oldsmobile owned by Springfield businessman Walter

Umenhofer, parked well over a quarter of a mile away from the explosion. The car's roof was completely caved in by a large slab of blubber. As he watched a highway worker remove the three-by-five foot hunk with a shovel, a stunned Umenhofer remarked, "My insurance company's never going to believe this."

The Aftermath
Down at the blast site, the only thing the dynamite had gotten rid of were

the seagulls. They were either scared away by the blast or repulsed by the awful stench, which didn't matter because most of the pieces of blubber lying around were far too large for them to eat. The beach was littered with huge chunks of ripe whale, including the whale's entire tail and a giant slab of mangled whale meat that never left the blast site. And the smell was actually worse than before. Thornton had hoped his work was done, but it was just beginning — he and his workers spent the rest of the day burying their mistake. His blunder drew the attention of news stations all over the country, but amazingly, he was promoted just six months later.

Twenty-five years later, the tale of the exploding whale is documented all over the Internet. And the Oregon Highway Division still gets calls about it today—many callers hoping to get their hands on the video. The whale is still dead, but the story took on a life of its own.

Dog Doo! Good God!

Palindromes are phrases or sentences
that are spelled the same way back-
ward and forward. Who comes up
with these things? Don't they have
jobs . . . or families . . . or any other
way to spend their time? Well,
whether they're weird or not, we're
hooked. Here are some of Uncle
John's favorites.

Ana, nab a banana.

Campus motto: Bottoms up, Mac!

Dog doo! Good God!

No, Mel Gibson is a casino's big lemon.

Pasadena, Ned — ASAP!

Straw? No, too stupid a fad. I put soot on warts.

Too far, Edna, we wander afoot.

He lived as a devil, eh?

Pull up, Eva, we're here! Wave! Pull up!

I saw desserts; I'd no lemons, alas no melon. Distressed was I.

Marge lets Norah see Sharon's telegram.

Ned, go gag Ogden.

No evil Shahs live on.

Myth-Conceptions

"Common knowledge" is frequently wrong. Here are some examples of things that many people believe . . . but that according to our sources, just aren't true.

Myth: "Give me a home where the buffalo roam, and the deer and the antelope play . . . "

Fact: There are no antelope in North America. The animal the song probably refers to is the pronghorn, which resembles an antelope. Real antelope only live in Asia and Africa.

Myth: The forbidden fruit eaten by Eve was an apple.
Fact: The Bible makes reference to the "fruit of the tree" (Genesis 3:3), but names no particular fruit. Horticulturists say that apple trees have never grown in the area where the Garden of Eden supposedly existed. She probably ate a pomegranate.

Myth: Hunger is triggered by an empty stomach.

Fact: Hunger is set off when nutrients are absent in the bloodstream. In response to this, the brain begins rhythmic contractions of the stomach and intestines, which causes stomach grumbling and the feeling of hunger.

Myth: A limb "falls asleep" because its blood supply gets cut off.

Fact: This feeling of numbness—called neurapraxia—happens when a major nerve is pinched against a hard object or bone. This causes the harmless temporary sensation of numbness, but the blood continues to flow normally.

Myth: Pandas are bears.
Fact: The red panda is an extremely large cousin of the raccoon (with the exception of the giant panda which is actually a bear!)

Survey Says . . .

Remember the Fast Money round on *Family Feud*? Answers come easily when you're sitting on your sofa . . . but imagine the pressure you'd feel on national television. You might even say something stupid.

Q: Name a fruit that is yellow.
A: Orange.

Q: Name something that floats in the bath.
A: Water.

Q: Name a famous cowboy.
A: Buck Rogers.

Q: A number you have to memorize.
A: Seven.

Q: Name a part of the body begin-ning with "N."
A: Knee.

Q: Something you do before going to bed.
A: Sleep.

Q: Name a bird with a long neck.
A: Naomi Campbell.

Q: Name something with a hole in it.
A: Window.

Q: Name a sign of the zodiac.
A: April.

Lucky Finds

Ever found something really valuable? It's one of the best feelings in the world. Here's another installment of a regular Bathroom Reader feature.

A Shaky Prospect
The Find: A dirty, moldy, wobbly old card table
Where It Was Found: At a lawn sale, for $25

The Story: In the late 1960s, a woman named Claire (no last name — she prefers to remain anonymous) moved to a new house and needed a small table for one of the rooms. She found one at a yard sale, but it was dirty and it wobbled; a friend advised against buying it, telling her that "it would never hold a lamp." She bought it anyway — after bargaining the price down from $30 to $25, because that was all the money she had in her purse. When she cleaned the table up, she noticed a label on the underside of it that read "John Seymour & Son Cabinet Makers Creek Square Boston." Claire did some research on it, but didn't learn a lot.

Nearly 30 years passed. Then in September 1997, Claire took her table to a taping of the PBS series *Antiques Roadshow*. There she learned that Seymour furniture is among the rarest and most sought-after in the United States; until Claire's table showed up, only five other pieces in original condition with the Seymour label were known to exist. Claire thought the table might be worth $20,000; the Antiques Roadshow appraiser put it at $300,000. Not even close—the table sold at auction at Sotheby's for $490,000.

A pretty good price for a table that can't hold a lamp.

I Yam What I Yam
The Find: A diamond
Where It Was Found: In Sierra

Leone . . . under a yam

The Story: In 1997 three hungry boys were scrounging for food near the village of Hinnah Malen in the African country of Sierra Leone. The boys, orphaned since 1995 when their parents had been killed in a rebel attack, had gone two days without food. They spent three unsuccessful hours searching for yams that morning and were on their way home when their luck changed. They found a yam under a palm tree and dug it up. Right under the yam they found a flawless 100-carat diamond. **Estimated value:** $500,000. "It was easy to see," according to the oldest boy, 14-year-old Morie Jah. "It was shining and sparkling."

Not Baa-aa-ad
The Find: A lost Hindu shrine
Where It Was Found: In a cave in the Himalayas, in India
The Story: In September 2001, a shepherd named Ghulam Qadir lost

some of his sheep and set out to look for them. He crawled into a small cave, thinking they might be there . . . but instead of his sheep, he found a 12-inch idol of the Hindu god Shiva. The cave turned out to be a 1,500-year-old shrine, one that had been forgotten and undisturbed for centuries. Government officials were so excited by the discovery that they have promised to pay Qadir 10% of the cash offerings left at the shrine from 2002 to 2007, followed by a large final payment when the five years are up. (He never did find his sheep.)

Unlucky Find
The Find: A swastika and a pile of pornographic magazines
Where They Were Found: In a brand-new Jaguar automobile — the magazines were stuffed into an interior cavity; the swastika was painted underneath a seat panel.
The Story: The discovery was made accidentally when the car was being

taken apart for bomb-proofing, because this car happened to be purchased by Queen Elizabeth. The magazines and the swastika were put there during assembly by an autoworker who had no idea of the car's final destination. "It is one of those old traditions where people used to write things behind the seat panel of cars and they were never discovered unless there was an accident," another factory worker told the British newspaper *The Guardian*, "only this time it wasn't funny."

Update: The worker responsible for the "factory extras" lost his job over the incident . . . but that probably won't stop the practice of hiding things in new cars. "The chaps go to an awful lot of trouble to do the car," says the Jaguar employee. "They're there all day. What else have they got to do?"

Strange Lawsuits

These days, it seems that people will sue each other over practically anything. Here are a few more real-life examples of unusual legal battles.

The Plaintiff: Janette Weiss
The Defendant: Kmart Corporation
The Lawsuit: Weiss was shopping for a blender. But the blenders were stacked on a high shelf, just out of her reach. Ignoring the laws of gravity,

Weiss jumped up and grabbed the bottom box. Predictably, when she yanked it out, the three blenders on top came crashing down on her head. Claiming to be suffering from "bilateral carpal-tunnel syndrome," Weiss sued Kmart for "negligently stacking the boxes so high on the upper shelf." **The Verdict:** Not guilty. After Weiss admitted on the stand that she knew the boxes would fall, it took the jury half an hour to find in favor of Kmart.

The Plaintiff: Dr. Ira Gore
The Defendant: BMW America
The Lawsuit: In 1990, Gore purchased a $40,000 BMW. After he got it home, he discovered that the dealer had touched up a scratch in the paint on a door and never bothered to tell him he was buying damaged goods. Outraged, Gore sued.
The Verdict: The jury awarded Gore $4,000 compensation, even though the actual repair cost only $600. And then they slapped BMW with an unbeliev-

able $2 million in punitive damages.

The Plaintiff: Jeffrey Stambovsky

The Defendant: Helen V. Ackley

The Lawsuit: Stambovsky purchased Ackley's house in Nyack, New York, for $650,000. When he later discovered that the house was "haunted," he sued Ackley for failing to disclose the presence of poltergeists.

The Verdict: Guilty. Unfortunately for her, Ackley had bragged to friends for years that the place was spooked. She was even interviewed by *Reader's*

Digest for an article on haunted houses. The judge found that Ackley should have told Stambovsky everything about the house, noting that the existence of ghosts meant that she had actually broken the law by not leaving the house vacant.

The Plaintiff: Chad Gabriel DeKoven

The Defendant: Michigan Prison System

The Lawsuit: DeKoven, a convicted

armed robber who goes by the name "Messiah-God," sued the prison system, demanding damages that included thousands of trees, tons of precious metals, peace in the Middle East, and "return of all U.S. military personnel to the United States within 90 days."

The Verdict: Case dismissed. While noting that all claims must be taken seriously, the judge ultimately dismissed the suit as frivolous. DeKoven, the judge said, "has no Constitutional right to be treated as the 'Messiah-God' or any other holy, extra-worldly or supernatural being."

The Plaintiff: Louis Berrios
The Defendant: Our Lady of Mercy Hospital
The Lawsuit: Berrios, a 32-year-old quadriplegic, entered the hospital complaining of stomach pains. Doctors took X-rays to determine the cause of his pain and then called the police when the film revealed what

they thought were bags of heroin in Berrios's stomach. The police interrogated Berrios and kept him handcuffed to a gurney for 24 hours, only to discover that the "bags of heroin" were actually bladder stones. Berrios, "shamed, embarrassed and extremely humiliated," sued the hospital for $14 million.

The Verdict: Unknown.

The Plaintiff: Judith Richardson Haimes

The Defendant: Temple University Hospital

The Lawsuit: Haimes claimed to have had psychic abilities . . . until a CAT scan at the Philadelphia hospital "destroyed her powers." The hospital's negligence left her unable to ply her trade as a clairvoyant, she said.

The Verdict: Amazingly, the jury awarded Haimes $986,465. The judge disagreed and threw out the verdict.

Fabulous Flops

Next time you see the hype for some amazing, "can't-niss" phenomenon, hold on to a healthy sense of skepticism by remembering these duds.

The National Bowling League
If people were willing to pay to watch professional football, baseball, and basketball teams, they'd pay to watch teams like the New York Gladiators and the Detroit Thunderbirds com-

pete against each other, right? That was the thinking behind the 10-team National Bowling League, founded in 1961. The owner of the Dallas Broncos poured millions of dollars into his franchise, building a special 2,500-seat "Bronco Bowl" with six lanes surrounded by 18 rows of seats arranged in a semicircle; space was also set aside for a seven-piece jazz band to provide entertainment between games. But he couldn't even fill the arena on opening night, and things went downhill after that. The league folded in less than a year.

Gerber Singles

This was Gerber Baby Food's attempt to sell food to adults. Launched in the 1970s, the line of gourmet entrees like sweet-and-sour pork and beef burgundy had two major problems: the food came in baby food-style jars, and the name "Singles" was a turnoff to customers who were lonely to begin with.

Hershey's Chocolate Soap

Milton Hershey didn't like to let anything go to waste. There were times in the chocolate business when he found himself with millions of pounds of cocoa butter that he didn't know what to do with, and he spent years trying to find a product that would put it to use. In the early 1930s, he finally settled on cocoa butter soap.

Three months later, the factory that he built behind the Cocoa Inn in Hershey, Pennsylvania, began pro-

ducing 120 bars of chocolate-scented
soap a minute. Finding 120 customers
a minute to buy the stuff proved to be
much more daunting. People were
used to eating their chocolate, not
bathing in it, and were put off by the
strong chocolate smell of the soap.
(Some even tried to eat the bars,
thinking they were candy.)

More than a million bars of the
stuff piled up in the basement of the
Hershey Sports Arena waiting to be
sold; nevertheless, Hershey kept the

assembly line running at full speed. "Don't worry about my money," he told his executives. "You just sell all you can." Seven years and several million dollars later, he finally pulled the plug. Ironically, cocoa butter—unscented—is a popular ingredient in soap today.

Solar-Powered Parking Meters
City officials in Nottingham, England, spent more than £1 million (about $1.5 million) installing solar-

powered parking meters on city
streets after reading reports that the
meters saved a fortune in mainte-
nance costs in Mediterranean
countries. The only problem:
Mediterranean countries get a lot of
sun . . . and England doesn't, not even
in summer. As of August 2001, more
than 25% of the parking meters were
out of commission, allowing hundreds
of motorists to park for free.

Hits Snack Food

One of the few products whose demise can be blamed solely on the packaging. When lined up end-to-end on store shelves, the packages read: "HITSHITSHITSHITSHITSHITSHITSHITS."

Looney Laws

Believe it or not, these laws are real.

In Tuscumbia, Alabama, it is against the law for more than eight rabbits to reside on the same block.

In Birmingham, Alabama, it is illegal to drive a car while blindfolded.

In Arizona it is illegal to hunt or shoot a camel.

In Atlanta it is illegal to make faces at school children while they are studying.

In Hawaii no one may whistle in a drinking establishment.

A law in Zion, Illinois, prohibits teaching household pets to smoke cigars.

According to Kentucky law, women may not appear on the highway in bathing suits unless they carry clubs.

In Marblehead, Massachusetts, each fire company responding to an alarm must be provided a three-gallon jug of rum.

It is illegal to fish for whales in any stream, river, or lake in Ohio.

Undertakers are prohibited from giving away books of matches in Shreveport, Louisiana.

It is unlawful to tie a crocodile to a fire hydrant in Detroit.

In Minnesota it is illegal to dry both men's and women's underwear on the same clothesline.

In Natchez, Mississippi, it is unlawful for elephants to drink beer.

It is illegal for barbers in Waterloo, Nebraska, to eat onions between 7 A.M. and 7 P.M.

In Yukon, Oklahoma, it is illegal for a patient to pull a dentist's tooth.

In Portland, Oregon, it is illegal to shake a feather duster in someone's face.

A South Carolina statute states that butchers may not serve on a jury when a man is being tried for murder.

In Knoxville, Tennessee, it is illegal to lasso a fish.

Urban Legends

Here's our latest batch of urban legends—have you heard any of these? Remember the BRI rule of thumb: If a wild story sounds a little too "perfect," it's probably an urban legend . . . or is it?

The Legend: Chocolate milk is made from tainted milk. Dairies too cheap to throw away unusable milk add chocolate to hide the bad taste.

How it Spread: This story started out as a schoolyard rumor, spread by kids. But it took on new life in the 1990s, when the introduction of pre-pared coffee drinks in bottles and cans inspired people to extend the children's tale to adult beverages.

The Truth: The milk in chocolate milk and coffee drinks is as carefully tested and regulated by the U.S. Food and Drug Administration as any other form of milk.

The Legend: When the Missouri Ku Klux Klan won a lengthy court battle to participate in the Adopt-a-Highway program—which would have required the state to use taxpayer dollars to "advertise" the KKK on those little roadside Adopt-a-Highway signs—the state legislature responded by naming the Klan's designated stretch of road after civil rights activist Rosa Parks.

How it Spread: By word of mouth and over the Internet.

The Truth: What makes this urban legend different from most others? It's true. In March 2000 the Missouri KKK really did win a legal battle to adopt a mile-long stretch of I-55 south of St. Louis, and the state legislature really did name it the Rosa Parks Highway in response.

Problem Solved: No one ever showed up to clean the road either before or after the name change, so the state dropped the KKK from the program in April 2000.

The Legend: A few years before the Gulf War, Barbara Walters did a news story on gender roles in Kuwait in which she reported that Kuwaiti wives traditionally walk several paces behind their husbands. She returned to Kuwait after the war and noticed that women were now walking several paces ahead of their husbands. When Walters asked a Kuwaiti woman how so much social progress had been accomplished in so little time, the woman replied, "Land mines."

How it Spread: By word of mouth and e-mail, starting shortly after the end of the Gulf War.

The Truth: This is the latest version of a classic urban legend that has been around as long as landmines themselves. The subjects of the story—Kuwaitis, Korean, and Vietnamese peasants, and in the case of World War II, nomads in North Africa—change to fit the circumstances of each new war.

The Legend: You can help oil-soaked Australian penguins by knitting tiny sweaters for them to wear and mailing them to an address in Tasmania, off the southern coast of Australia.

How it Spread: By word of mouth, e-mail, and cable news broadcasts, following an oil spill near Tasmania on New Year's Day 2000.

The Truth: Another example of an urban "legend" that's actually true. This one is a request for public assistance that snowballed out of control.

In 2001 the Tasmanian Conservation Trust and State Library asked knitters to put their leftover yarn to good use by knitting it into penguin sweaters. It even posted a pattern on the Internet so that knitters would know how to make one in just the right shape and size. (The sweaters keep oil-soaked penguins warm and prevent them from ingesting oil until they regain enough strength to be scrubbed clean.)

The story received international

news coverage, prompting concerned knitters all over the world to begin sending penguin sweaters to Tasmania. The Conservation Trust had hoped to create a stockpile of 100 in preparation for the next oil spill, but more than 800 arrived in the first few weeks alone; from there the number just kept growing. "They're all one size," says a volunteer. "But at least the penguins have a choice of color."

The Price Was Right

You've heard people talk about how much things cost back in the "good old days"—heck, you might even remember them yourself (Uncle John does). Talk about nostalgia . . . check out these prices.

1900:
Seven-shot revolver: $1.25
Bicycle: $20
Grand piano: $175

Men's leather belt: 19¢

Alligator bag: $5

1910:

All-expenses-paid trip to Bermuda for nine days: $37.50

Bottle of Coke: 5¢

Imported spaghetti: 12¢/box

Cigarettes: 10¢/pack

Wage for postal workers: 42¢/hr.

1920:

Life insurance premium: $16.40/yr.

Chocolates: 89¢/lb.

Eggs: 64¢/doz.

Box of 50 cigars: $2.98

Public school teacher's salary: $970/yr.

1930:

Christmas tree light set (eight bulbs): 88¢

Electric toaster: $1

Motor oil. 49¢/gal.

Washing machine: $58

1940:

Coffeemaker: $2

Movie ticket: 25¢ (day); 40¢ (night)

Golf balls: $1.88/doz.

Bayer aspirin: 59¢

Minimum wage: 30¢/hr.

1950:

Jackie Robinson's salary ('51):
    $39,750/yr.

Roll of film: 38¢

Toilet paper (20 rolls): $2.39

Corvette ('53): $3,498

Combination 19" television/FM radio/
phonograph: $495

1960:
Refrigerator: $200
Polaroid Camera: $100
Mercedes Benz 220S: $3,300
Breakfast (two hot cakes and two
    strips of bacon): 33¢
Clearasil: 98¢/tube

1970:
Answering machine: $50

Sirloin steak: 97¢/lb.
Tennis racket: $25
Movie projector: $80
Orange juice: 35¢/qt.

1980:
Cordless telephone: $300
Six-pack of Budweiser: $1.99
Video camera: $360
Cadillac El Dorado: $19,700

Behind the Hits

Ever wonder what inspired some of your favorite songs? Here are a few more inside stories about popular tunes.

The Artist: Beck
The Song: "Loser"
The Story: One day, Beck was fooling around at producer Karl Stephenson's house. Beck started

playing slide guitar, and Stephenson began recording. As Stephenson added a Public Enemy–style beat and a sample from Dr. John's "I Walk on Gilded Splinters," Beck attempted to freestyle rap—something he had never done before. Frustrated at his inability to rap, Beck began criticizing his own performance: "Soy un perdedor." ("I'm a loser" in Spanish.) Beck wanted to scrap it, but Stephenson thought it was catchy. Stephenson was right—"Loser" made Beck a star.

The Artist: David Bowie

The Song: "Fame"

The Story: In 1975, as Bowie and his band were playing around in the studio with a riff that guitarist Carlos Alomar had come up with, former Beatle John Lennon dropped in. When they played the riff for Lennon, he immediately picked up a guitar, walked to the corner of the room and started playing along and muttering to himself, "Aim . . . aim!" When he said, "Fame!" the song started to come together. Bowie ran off to write some lyrics while the band worked out the music. Bowie gave writing credit to Lennon, saying: "It wouldn't have happened if John hadn't been there."